# KING OF THE HILL

## A Child's Personal History of the Great Depression

*by*

Nelda Bedford Gaydou

*Illustrated by Sabrina Bedford*

No part of this publication may be reproduced, stored in a retrieval system, or transmitted in any form or by any means, electronic, mechanical, photocopying, recording, or otherwise, without the written permission of the publisher.

Text Copyright © 2018 Nelda Bedford Gaydou

All rights reserved.
Published 2018 by
Progressive Rising Phoenix Press, LLC
www.progressiverisingphoenix.com

ISBN: 978-1-946329-68-4

Printed in the U.S.A.
1st Printing

Edited by Dr. David A. Bedford

Illustrations, cover image and layout by Sabrina Bedford
Visit www.msgbedford.com

## Table of Contents

About This Book..................................................i
At the Caprock..................................................1
Pulling Cotton..................................................7
The Three R's..................................................11
Third Time's the Charm..................................15
Elbow Grease..................................................19
No Job Too Big or Too Small..........................25
King of the Hill..............................................31
Changes..........................................................37
Excursions......................................................41
Twists and Turns............................................47
Study Guide....................................................49
About the Author..........................................64

# ABOUT THIS BOOK

I grew up hearing stories about my parents' childhood, which was probably a lot like that of your great-grandparents. In the 1930s the world was quite different from yours and mine. It was during the Great Depression, when most families in the U.S. were very poor.

My father was the youngest of eleven children, three of whom had died before he was even born. My grandfather, son of a Texas Ranger, grew up ranching and farming. He married my grandmother in eastern Oklahoma when it was still Indian Territory. They also lived in Arizona, New Mexico and Texas, working at whatever they could: farming, mining, shopkeeping and a wide variety of odd jobs.

When the stories in this book took place, the Bedfords were farming. They had practically no money and living conditions were very basic. What stands out for me from my father's memories is that he had such a happy childhood, with his large close family and kind neighbors. I'm amazed by the ingenuity with which they got everything done and by how much fun they had along the way in spite of their troubles.

I hope you enjoy these stories and learn as much from them as I always have!

# AT THE CAPROCK

Benji was curious and excited. He didn't know exactly what was going on, but he was sure it was an adventure.

"Are we really leaving tomorrow, Ira?"

"Mm-hmm."

"Where are we going?"

"Paducah, Texas."

"Why?"

"Papa heard they're hiring people to pick cotton."

"So?"

"Papa can't find work here."

"What do you mean? He works all the time!"

"But they're all odd jobs."

"Odd?"

"Not strange, just odds and ends, not a regular, full-time job."

"Oh."

The next day he buzzed around as the family loaded up the truck. When everything was ready, he climbed into the back and squeezed in with Papa, Mama, Mary, Jewel, Ira, their dog Fritz and their pet rabbit. Troy and L.D. were in the cab to take turns driving. It was crowded there, too, with L.D.'s wife and their two little girls. A.T. and Billie, the only Bedfords with steady jobs, stayed behind.

It was summer and, as they crossed the state line from New Mexico into Texas, the sun shone bright and hot, but they were protected by a big sheet of canvas over the top and sides of the wooden truck bed. They sat on bedrolls propped against bundles of clothes and between kitchen utensils as they bumped along the road. When they got to Lubbock, they found an empty field and camped out under the stars.

In the morning, they piled back into the truck. Although Paducah was only a little over one hundred miles away, it would take several hours to get there. The fastest a Model T could go was forty to forty-five miles per hour, but this one was old and heavily loaded, so it crawled along quite a bit more slowly than that.

Soon they were swaying around curves, going up and down hill after hill. They had entered the Caprock Escarpment, a land carved out by the White River over countless years. The ground was broken into gullies, ditches and canyons. Sandy, chocolate and red soils showed through scrubby grass. Juniper, cactus and mesquite added dusty shades of green.

The poor truck struggled up each hill, until one really steep rise was too much for it. Not only could it not keep going forward—it began rolling back down, picking up speed as it went.

"Hang on!" someone yelled as those in the back tumbled around among the pots and pans.

Before they sailed into a gully, L.D. pulled on the steering wheel and backed the truck into a ditch on the right side of the road, where it came to a crunching halt against the bank.

"Oh, no!" shouted Benji.

The rabbit had jumped out and was hopping across the grass. The dog barked madly and scrambled after it, closely followed by Ira and Benji. Fritz finally caught the rabbit and pinned it down—he knew better than to try to eat it.

By the time they got back, everyone was out of the truck.

"How much money do we have?" asked Papa.

They emptied their pockets and counted. There were five dollars in all, and that's what it took to have the truck pulled out of the ditch.

The men discussed what to do next.

"Maybe it can make it without such a heavy load."

Everyone waited at the side of the road while Troy got in the driver's seat and gave it another try. He was almost all the way up when the truck started shaking and coughing. It stopped and began to slide back down. Troy kept it as straight as he could to avoid falling into another ditch. Finally, the truck stopped right at the brink of a deep gully and refused to start up again.

Two young men drove up and stopped to see what had happened and why there was such a crowd. L.D. took his pistol out of its holster and held it out to them as he asked, "Can you tow us to the next town?"

"Whatever you say!" they stammered, backing away.

"I'm sorry! I didn't mean to scare you. This is the only thing I can pay you with."

"Oh, okay," they laughed in relief.

They all climbed back into the truck and the young men towed them thirteen miles to the nearest town, which was Dickens. While the rest of the family set up camp, Papa walked over to the General Store. They now had no money and nothing to eat but a bit of day-old bread. Mama had not been able to wash the skillet after their last meal on the road, so it still had some grease from the sausage they had fried, and it gave the bread a little flavor when they toasted it in the skillet over an open fire.

Papa finally returned. He had met a farmer who agreed to hire the family to pull cotton in his fields and allow them to live on the farm. The next morning the farmer towed the Model T to the barn and let them into the house. That is how the Bedfords ended up in Dickens County instead of Paducah.

# PULLING COTTON

Although he was only five and the youngest in the family, Benji didn't want to miss anything, even if it meant working. It was time to start harvesting cotton, so he got up very early, while it was still dark. He shrugged into a shirt and pulled on his overalls. After a breakfast of biscuits and sausage, he put on shoes, hat and gloves.

"I'm ready!" he announced.

Papa grinned and held out a surprise: his very own cotton sack, just like the others except smaller. He showed his little son how to put his head and one arm through the strap so that the sack hung at his side and behind him, leaving his hands free. When they got to the field they fanned out, one on each row, and started moving forward at the same time.

In this case, they were pulling rather than picking. Picking cotton meant pinching only the white fibers out from the boll, the pod that holds the cotton and seeds. Pulling cotton meant yanking off the entire boll and stuffing it into the sack. If the bolls were close enough, they could pull several at the same time by lacing their fingers through the stems. When the bags were full, they were taken to a trailer and weighed on scales before being emptied into a big wire cage. There was a sheet of paper for writing down the weight of each bag beside the name of the person who had pulled the cotton, because they got paid by the pound. The more they pulled, the more they got paid. The process was repeated until the cage was full. Then they took it to the cotton gin, a machine that separated out cotton for fabric, seeds for oil and bolls for fertilizer. This went on until all the cotton was harvested.

After a while, Benji would fall behind his parents and older siblings. Whenever this happened, Troy, who worked beside him, would pull a bunch of bolls loose on his little brother's row so that he could stuff them into his sack quickly and catch up again. Since Benji couldn't write yet, one of the others would jot down his weights for him. At the end of the day he would amaze his family by remembering the exact amount of cotton pulled by each person. It turned out that Jewel was the fastest of them all.

When the Bedfords finished harvesting all the cotton at the Stevens Place, they offered their services at neighboring farms. If they were not within walking distance, they rode a horse-drawn cart. The cotton harvest season started in late summer and went on through the fall. That year, 1932, the children did not start school in September because all hands were needed in the fields. It was hard work, but they were happy—they were earning their food and the roof over their heads.

# THE THREE R'S

Benji climbed onto the bus, looked around, and sat down beside the little redheaded girl from the neighbors' ranch. One of the bigger boys started chanting, making fun of the new kid. Before he could decide what to say or do, his friend swung her lunch pail right at the bully's head, connecting with a loud whack. There was no more teasing.

The Dickens school was in a ten-room, two-story brick building. Benji was assigned a locker and shown to his classroom. He sat where he was told and tried to blend in. When the bell rang, he dashed to his locker, ready to eat. The other children laughed and stopped him:

"It's not lunchtime yet. It's recess. Come play!"

Although he started school late because he had to work in the fields during the cotton harvest, Benji was not behind. In fact, he was moved up from Lower to Upper First when the teachers discovered that he could already add, subtract and read. He had become good with numbers by keeping track of the rows and furrows, stacks and bags in the cotton fields, but he wasn't really sure how he had learned to read. It just happened.

For a long time, the two youngest Bedford brothers had followed a nightly ritual. Benji loved stories so much that he traded them for chores and kept close count ("You still owe me two stories!"). The boys saved pennies from odd jobs until they got together ten cents—enough to buy the first of the exciting new series of Big Little Books. It was called *The Adventures of Dick Tracy*, a collection of stories about a detective whose favorite gadget was a radio-wristwatch. The books were 3 6/8" wide, 4 1/2" high, about 1 1/2" thick, and from 212 to 432 pages long. The text was on the left, with black-and-white illustrations on the right. At some point, Benji began to connect the words Ira read with the printed letters on the page. Now he just had to learn to write.

Benji got out of class before his brother and sister, so he had time to play with his new friends. They went up and down the streets of Dickens, past the little windmill on the Courthouse lawn, the white brick box that housed the Sheriff's Office and the County Jail, and the General Store.

Because he got out earlier than the others, Benji often ran the family errands. One day his mother had asked him to get vinegar because they were having company and she wanted to bake a vinegar pie. While he and his friends were waiting for the upper grades to be let out, Benji entertained them by imitating the teacher. Unfortunately, he dropped the quart glass jug, which shattered on the ground. He rushed up the stairs to Ira's classroom and had him called out.

"What should I do?"

"Just go back and get another one. I won't say anything."

Benji raced back to the store and asked for another jug of vinegar. Ira used this against him for a long time. Whenever he wanted to make his little brother do something, he would threaten him by simply murmuring, "Vinegar, vinegar!"

If he had only told his mother what happened, Benji would have known that she had been aware of the second jug since the very next grocery bill. This was because he didn't pay with cash: the storekeeper had a notebook where he wrote down what the little boy took, and his parents paid at the end of the month.

# THIRD TIME'S THE CHARM

The stovepipe sat uneasily on top of the pile of household belongings, leaning more and more with each turn of the wheels over the dirt road. Finally, it slid right off, bouncing and rolling away. Ira and Benji jumped off the wagon and ran after it.

"Thanks, boys!" said Papa. He had practically grown up in the saddle, herding cattle in the Texas Hill Country, and never learned to drive a car or truck. He much preferred leading a team of horses or mules. The family was moving again because they had a new sharecropping agreement, farming in exchange for housing and part of the crops.

Dickens County was a collection of farms and ranches grouped around small towns. Spur and Dickens were the largest, and most of the others consisted of not much more than a church, a filling station and a store. Individual holdings were known as "places," identified by the owner's name. The Bedfords had lived at the Stevens Place for one season and the Gilstrap Place for about one year. Now they were headed for the Reynolds Place.

The first house had been quite small, with only two bedrooms: Mama and Papa in one, L.D. and his family in the other, while everyone else slept on pallets on the screened-in porch. The Gilstrap Place, halfway between Dickens and Afton, was somewhat larger, but didn't have a storm cellar, so Papa and the older sons had to dig one. When bad weather came, they all got in and Papa pulled down and fastened shut the big sheet of wood that was both door and roof until it was safe to leave. They also used the cellar to store canned goods and keep them cool and fresh.

The owner's house was not far from theirs and the younger boys soon made friends with the daughter. Ira liked her and was always looking for ways to impress her. One day he was showing off by racing around the top of the cement wall that surrounded their neighbors' water tank when he lost his balance and fell in with a loud splash.

"Don't tell anyone, Benji! Please don't tell," begged a very embarrassed Ira, while he waited for his clothes to dry off before going home, hoping no one would notice.

"I won't if you call off the Vinegar-Vinegar deal," answered his little brother between fits of laughter.

They shook hands on it.

The house was half a mile from the highway, where the kids could catch the bus on school days, and Jewel's best friend lived across the road. Since getting anywhere involved a lot of walking, they often took shortcuts across the fields. One of the most useful was through the pie melons. These small, round relatives of the watermelon lay scattered on the ground and were used to feed the cows and pigs. Benji hated crossing the field alone because it was a favorite hangout for snakes, including rattlers. He hurried across, keeping his eyes peeled. If he saw one very near, he would chuck a rock at it and, in all cases, run as fast as his legs would carry him.

But when he was with Papa, he felt safe. Every Sunday they would walk to church through the fields and by the highway that was under construction. The workers marked out their path with binder twine, and left it behind when they moved on to pave the next stretch of road. Papa would often pick up the twine, roll it up into a neat ball and drop it in his pocket—it was sure to come in handy.

# ELBOW GREASE

The Reynolds Place, located near Croton, had quite a bit more room than their previous houses. Although it was now rather run down, it must have been very comfortable and advanced when it was built. The remains of fancy gas fittings could still be seen but, just like the others, it had no electricity, no gas and no running water.

During the day lighting came from the sun and at night from kerosene lamps. The base of the lamp was the fuel tank or fount. A cotton wick absorbed the kerosene and gave off light as it burned. A glass chimney sat on top of the base to protect the wick, keep the flame from being blown out and allow the right amount of air in to keep it going, and there was a handle for carrying or hanging. The best one was the Aladdin Lamp, whose manufacturer offered $1,000 to anyone who could show a lamp that worked better. The prize was never collected.

Wood and dry cow chips were the fuel for cooking and heating. Once Papa got a job grubbing a field, which meant digging out the stumps and roots of the mesquite trees that had been chopped down. Part of the deal was keeping the stumps for fuel. Ira and Benji helped load them onto the wagon, their heads protected by blue felt hats that someone had given them before they left New Mexico. Tom and Burton, Troy's future stepsons, were on a visit from Clovis and went along as well, since they were about the same age as their soon-to-be uncles. On the way home, they entertained themselves by snatching Benji's hat off his head and tossing it on the ground. After hopping off and on the wagon several times, he managed to get a strong grip the next time they grabbed. This strategy was only partly successful: when they yanked, the crown of the hat ripped away, leaving only the brim clinging snugly to his head.

Of course, the family needed to be careful with the wood. The stove could be tricky and often flared up. One day while they were outside waiting for the school bus, the children saw black smoke rolling off the roof and raced back to help. Another morning the stove caught fire while Mama was preparing breakfast. She had just cut out the biscuits when the flames leapt out, and she dropped the pan on the floor. In the confusion, she stepped in the middle of it with her bare feet. Once the fire had been put out, she calmly picked up the pan and slid it into the oven. She wasn't about to let that good food go to waste, but the biscuits certainly had a strange shape that day.

Every bit of water they used had to be carried into the house in a bucket from a tank that was fed from the well by a windmill. No running water meant no indoor toilets. A hole was dug, and an outhouse built over it some distance from the house. Catalogues from Sears Roebuck Co. and Montgomery Ward did double duty for reading and cleaning. Washed and dried corn cobs were also used as toilet paper. A bag of white lime powder was kept nearby, and a scoopful was added to the hole from time to time to kill the bacteria and their odor. It did such a good job of this that the waste did not get broken down and the hole eventually filled up. At that point, a new hole would have to be dug nearby. The dirt from the new pit would be placed on top of the old one, and the outhouse would be moved over the new hole.

Washing clothes was a complicated process. There was a popular song among the little girls at that time: "Monday is wash day at our house; we're happy as can be. I wash clothes for my dolly, while Mommy scrubs for me!" That sounded like fun, but actually it was very hard work. A large heavy iron tub was set on blocks, filled with water, and heated by a wood fire underneath. White clothes were washed first, and the order of the rest depended on how soiled they were. After being boiled to loosen the dirt, they were scrubbed on wooden washboards with metal ridges, using soap made at home from lard. Then they were dipped in a starch solution and hung on the line to dry. The next day they were sprinkled with water and rolled up to dampen evenly. The flat iron was heated on the cook stove or over an open fire and everything was ironed, except underwear and socks.

Saturday was the usual day for bathing by immersion. Round metal tubs big enough to sit in were partly filled with cold water and brought to bathing temperature with kettles of boiling water. Afterwards, the dirty water had to be hauled back outside because there were no drains. But when it was warm they bathed outside. A showerhead was placed on the pipe that ran down from the tank, and a makeshift canvas stall provided privacy.

# NO JOB TOO BIG OR TOO SMALL

"Uh-oh! I can feel the first drops. Hurry, Benji, get in the barn before the storm breaks!" yelled Papa. He and the others were spread out across the field and started making their way back.

Benji shook the reins and urged the team of four horses forward. At seven years of age, he was the official farm equipment driver, freeing up the older family members for heavier manual labor. The year before, when it was time to harvest maize at the Gilstrap Place, Benji had learned to drive the sled cutter. It was his job to guide two horses in a straight line so that the sharp blades on either side would cut through the plants. As the others went down the furrows, the first ones grabbed armfuls of the crop and dropped them on the ground. Those behind formed bundles, bound them and stacked them. If there was danger of rain or hail ruining the crop, they even worked at night, by moonlight.

Now he was driving the cultivator. It had two large metal wheels that looked like they belonged to a giant bicycle. Metal rods held a bare frame together and, from a bright orange seat high in the middle, Benji had to keep it moving straight, so that the forks churned and loosened up the dirt alongside the plants without pulling them up, and the blades cut down the weeds between the furrows.

The horses barely made it into the barn before it began pouring. Benji removed the harnesses as he pictured everyone else getting soaked through and through. He looked out into the moving wall of water, waiting impatiently: they were having an adventure and he was just standing there, bored! So, he stepped out from under cover and got drenched just like the others.

The family took on just about any work that came their way. Among other things, Papa was hired to dig a well after a dowser, or water finder, had walked all around the field holding out a Y-shaped branch called a divining rod. When it finally pointed down, the dowser said, "This is the spot, Mr. Bedford!" Papa was paid with a mare and a colt. Except for the mare, which was sold for money, and the colt, which became the younger boys' pet, the work animals belonged to the farmer. The Bedfords could use them but they were responsible for their care. Every morning before leaving for school the children helped feed the horses, mules, cows, pigs and chickens; milk the cows; and gather eggs.

One of Benji's odd jobs was helping the iceman with his deliveries from time to time in exchange for a few pennies or ice. In and around Dickens, the iceman drove a blue pickup. He wore a leather apron and slung a sack over his shoulder to protect it from the blocks he carried from the icehouse to his truck and from there to his customers' iceboxes. His tools were wires, hooks, tongs and icepicks. Usually, people didn't want whole blocks, so the iceman would mark and split them into fourths with amazing skill.

Most houses had iceboxes, made of wood and standing on legs. They had hollow walls lined with tin or zinc and packed with materials such as cork, sawdust, straw or seaweed to keep in the cold. A large block of ice was fed from the top into a tray or compartment, and the cold air from the ice made its way down and around the rest of the storage area and its shelves. Food items were put in and taken out through doors on the front. The fancier models had taps for draining the ice water from a catch pan or holding tank, while for simpler models drip pans were placed underneath and had to be emptied at least once per day.

Ice was also an essential ingredient for one of Benji's favorite treats: ice cream. The only bought items it required were ice and salt. The ice cream maker was a tall wooden ice bucket, kept moist to prevent cracking. It had a handle for turning a metal container inside the bucket and a paddle inside the container for mixing the content. Papa loved ice cream and was in charge of the entire process. Benji would sit by his side listening to his father's stories and waiting for the chance to lick the paddle clean. The usual flavor was vanilla, but it could be changed according to the fruit on hand and, as an extra-special treat, there was chocolate. Sometimes Mama baked a cake to go along with it. The whole family would gather and often the neighbors were invited to share while they talked and laughed.

Money was so scarce that everything possible was grown or prepared at home. Store-bought items were limited to things like flour, cornmeal, sugar, salt and baking powder. Many of these products came in twenty-five or fifty-pound cotton bags. Several years before, the sacks began appearing in different colors when it became clear that they were being used as sewing material. Hard-to-wash-out stamps were replaced by easy-to-remove paper labels. Competition grew as the brands chosen by the customers began to depend more and more on the sacks' prints. Some even came with patterns for dresses, dolls, stuffed animals and quilt blocks. To save on footwear, rubber half soles could be bought to repair worn-down shoes, but when money was too tight for that, cardboard did the trick.

# KING OF THE HILL

"Three geese flying south with old Southall in their mouths; when they found they had a fool, they dropped him off at Patton Springs Grammar School," chanted a mischievous group of children. Now that they lived near Croton, Benji, Ira and Jewel began attending class in Afton, where a building was under way for the four hundred pupils from the old Afton, Midway, Croton, Wichita, Duncan Flat and Prairie Chapel school districts, now consolidated into one. Until construction was complete, extra classrooms were improvised in the neighborhood church buildings. O.C. Southall was the first superintendent.

Benji made new friends and learned new games. The whole class would often play "Red Rover, Red Rover." Two teams with the same number of persons would line up opposite each other, no more than thirty feet apart, and form a chain by linking arms. The teams took turns calling one player from the other team: "Red Rover, Red Rover send (Name) on over!" That person would run to the other line and try to break through. Failure meant joining the team that had called. Success meant capturing one of the players at the broken link and returning with the captive to the original team. The game ended when all the players were on one side. They really got into the spirit of the thing, too, and went as far as tackling their classmates to prevent them from making it to the other team's line.

Apples were a favorite snack at recess. When one of the boys finished his fruit, he would yell, "Apple core!" The others all tried to be the first to answer, "Baltimore!" The winner was asked, "Who's your friend?" and the apple core was thrown at the one named, shouting, "Not no more!" Benji had never heard of the city named Baltimore, and for a long time he thought they were saying "Bottle o' more."

Benji also enjoyed spirited games of marbles. One day he was really on a roll and had won a whole bagful from his opponents. He was working on getting back his favorite starter, an Agate (the best marble brand), when a shadow fell over the circle in the dirt. It was Ira.

"What do you think you're doing?! You can't play for keeps! Give those marbles back right this minute!" Benji not only lost the bagful but his trusty Agate as well.

From the Stevens Place, the boys had been within walking distance of Dickens Peak, and they often raced each other and their friends to the top. If there were several of them, they would form a circle and try to catch a rabbit before it bolted down a hole.

Now a favorite pastime was King of the Hill. A creek bed, which was dry most of the year, ran through the Reynolds Place, at the foot of a sandy bank. The boys would strip down to their underwear, put their clothes in a pile out of harm's way, and troop up to the top. Then they wrestled, pulled and pushed each other until, one by one, they lost their balance and rolled down the smooth bank. The last one standing was "King of the Hill," but it was just as much fun (or more) to lose as to win.

Sundays were the best days for recreation. The Bedfords attended Friendship Baptist Church in the morning, and the rest of the day was for resting and playing. In the summer all the neighborhood children went swimming in Croton, in the big earthen tank that had a windmill and was used to water the livestock. It was also where Mama, Ira and Benji were baptized. A spectacular thunderstorm marked the occasion when it was Ira's turn.

The families from the surrounding farms often took turns gathering at each other's houses for potluck suppers, where everyone brought a dish to share. When funds had to be raised for a community project, they organized pie suppers, also called box socials. People would bid on the boxes, whose contents were hidden, and invite someone to eat the surprise meal with them. Many found it the perfect occasion for a first date.

The kids frequently held their own version of a rodeo, which consisted mainly of taking turns roping and riding young horses and calves, cheering when they stayed on and laughing when they fell off. Before one of these, there was exciting news: there was an unbroken colt and some of the children thought it would be the perfect attraction at their next event.

"I bet you wouldn't ride it, Benji!" challenged one of them. They all knew that their friend seldom turned down a dare, so they held their breath expectantly.

"I'll do it!" said Benji, and he was just sticking out his hand to seal the bargain when it got yanked back.

"Oh, no you won't! Are you crazy or what?" demanded Ira. Once again, Benji was foiled or saved by his big brother, depending on the point of view.

# CHANGES

Benji's family was changing. L.D. moved to Spur with his wife and little girls. In Clovis, weddings were in the air: Billie had married and settled down to run a store, Mary moved back and got engaged, and Troy would soon be tying the knot with a widow who lived there. But the core remained the same: home was where Mama and Papa were.

Although Benji had never thought of him as being old, at sixty-seven Papa was the same age as most of his friends' grandfathers. Except for driving cars, it seemed that there was nothing he couldn't do: kind and gentle, strong and resourceful, he had never given up on anyone or anything. They could always count on Papa.

The three and a half years of hard work in Texas were finally paying off and now the Bedfords were all settling into their new routines. Then one cold December evening a nasty cough sounded throughout the house. It was Papa and, once he started, he couldn't stop. When spots of blood appeared on his handkerchief, Troy insisted on driving him and Mama to the doctor in Spur. He returned alone with very bad news. Papa had tuberculosis and it was too late to do anything about it. He was so sick that he was unable to leave L.D.'s house.

Troy sent word to the others in Clovis and then drove Jewel, Ira and Benji to Spur. By the time the rest of the family joined them, L.D.'s little house was bursting at the seams. Troy's girlfriend Sue looked after the younger children and helped them set up pallets, so they could sleep on the floor. In the middle of the night she woke them up and called them to their father's bedside. They all crowded around Papa. He smiled at the faces that he loved so much and then he was gone.

He was buried in the Spur cemetery next to his baby granddaughter, who had passed away only a year before. Many friends and relatives came to say goodbye. Now Mama proved that she was just as strong as her husband had been. Although her heart was broken, she took charge. There was still a year and a half left on their sharecropping contract at the Reynolds Place. She would keep things going from day to day with the children who still lived at home, and her older sons and nephews would come from Clovis to help bring in the crops at harvest time.

# EXCURSIONS

Sometimes Benji thought that Ira took being a big brother a bit too far. Not only that, now that he considered himself the man of the house, he took the responsibilities that he felt went with it very seriously indeed.

Although he was only thirteen, Mama had Ira learn to drive the family's Ford V8. Troy gave him lessons before moving to Clovis, while Benji watched and listened from the back seat. Ira concentrated so hard that he would get stiff all over. He kept stalling the engine and the car jerked and jumped forward as he tried to work the clutch, brake and gas pedals with his feet, and the steering wheel and stick shift with his hands. It was absolutely infuriating for him that when his nine-year-old brother finally wheedled a turn out of Troy, the car glided smoothly along from gear to gear.

Of course, Ira finally got the hang of it and became an excellent driver. One day the car had to be taken to Spur for some minor repairs. Naturally, Benji tagged along for the ride and the chance to do something different in town.

"Let's go to the movies!" he suggested hopefully. "We can hitch a ride back home. There's always someone here from Croton on Saturdays."

"No, we can't take the chance. Let's go!"

They began the long fifteen-mile walk home. Soon a neighbor and his family passed them on their way to an outing in Spur. The boys had covered about ten miles when the neighbors overtook them on the way back and offered them a ride. To Benji's relief, Ira accepted, and they got out at the neighbors' house with two more miles to cover on foot.

Benji did make one trip on his own. That was when he had to go to Clovis to have his tonsils removed. Jess Terry, the pastor who preached at their church every other weekend, took him as far as the drugstore in Farwell, right on the border between Texas and New Mexico. There Benji caught a ride on in to Clovis, where he had his operation and stayed with Billie until he was well enough to go home. His big brother A.T. returned with him. A truck driver who made deliveries for their brother-in-law dropped them off at a creamery in Lubbock. He told them that for a quarter they could spend the night at the local YMCA, but neither A.T. nor Benji had a quarter so they dozed on benches inside the big building until daylight. Then they caught a ride to Dickens and walked the last six miles to the Reynolds Place.

The next Christmas, Jewel and Ira took turns driving the car. One of its interesting features was that the front doors hinges were on the center posts so that they opened from the front instead of the middle. Whenever she felt that the drivers were going too fast, Mama would say, "I think you're getting a little too merry!" They were on their way to Odessa, where L.D. now lived. He had a trucking business, hauling mud for the oil company. His partner and neighbor, Lloyd Allison, used to live near the Bedfords in Dickens. His son "Speedy" was about Benji's age and generously lent him his bicycle so he could learn to ride. In the process, he took quite a tumble and got a big lump on his head, but it was worth it!

Grandmother Anthony, Mama's mother, took turns living with her sons in Oklahoma and New Mexico. During one of her stays in Oklahoma, she became quite ill. Uncle "Naysh" (Ignatius) and his son J.P. rode a bus from Clovis to join Mama and the children in Dickens, and they all travelled on together. Jewel was annoyed that J.P. hogged so much of the driving time. On the way, they were the victims of a hit-and-run accident. The trucker who sideswiped them did not stop. None of them were hurt but the car was not as lucky.

They were forced to stay for several weeks because they had no way to get home. Grandmother Anthony recovered, and the family used the time to work in the nearby fields and earn a little money. The boys heard an old family story and wondered if they would find buried treasure.

Long ago their Uncles George, Crawford and Henry, who like Mama were one-fourth Choctaw, had come across some old Indian relics on their land when they were farming with Papa. At first, they hung them from a rafter in the roof. Then they decided to bury them for safekeeping and there they remained for a very long time. Years later the family wondered if the relics might not be valuable enough to help them out of their financial troubles, but they were unable to find them. A man who owned a metal detector made a trip with Papa to search the land for the buried cache. The understanding was that he would get a commission if they found anything, which they didn't. Neither did the boys. Some of the family suspected that George's good fortune in Oregon might have had something to do with the mysterious disappearance of the relics.

Eventually, relatives from Clovis made the trip to Oklahoma and took the Bedfords back to Dickens County. The car was retrieved later on, when the repairs had been completed and paid for.

# TWISTS AND TURNS

Mama and the children managed their farming duties with occasional out-of-town help. Even Troy's stepsons Tom and Burton and their grandfather pitched in.

Mr. Hammond chewed tobacco, and Benji and Tom noticed that he stashed his rope-like twist on a rafter in the back porch. The boys were fascinated and waited for their chance to sample it. The first time they had the place to themselves, they climbed up, retrieved the twist of tobacco, pulled off a piece each, and began chewing. It was unsweetened and, as far as Benji was concerned, tasted horrible. In his haste to spit it out, he accidentally swallowed a mouthful. He had an awful day out in the field. When he wasn't throwing up, he felt the ground heaving beneath him, while the rows and furrows seemed to wave up and down beside him. He was never tempted to try chewing tobacco again.

When the last of the crops had been harvested and the contract had been successfully completed, Mama felt that it was time to join the rest of the family in New Mexico. Benji was sorry to say goodbye to his friends and the places where he had loved to play, but he was also looking forward to new adventures.

Mama planned the move just in time for the green bean harvest in Portales. Betty the cow and Ira, who was now in junior high, stayed with Billie while the others spent several weeks picking beans and earning a few extra dollars before renting a small house in Clovis. Benji was enrolled in the sixth grade at La Casita, the same elementary school that several of his siblings had attended years ago.

Now they were surrounded by brothers and sisters, aunts and uncles, first cousins and second cousins, and a bunch of other relatives. From then on, they had electricity, running water and indoor bathrooms. Although he missed the wide, open spaces of Dickens County, Benji soon got used to life in town and picked up a whole new set of odd jobs: a weekend paper route, caddying at the golf course, selling fruit and vegetables door to door, and stacking shelves in the supermarket. After five years, the Texas chapter of his life was over, but what a chapter it had been!

# Study Questions for KING OF THE HILL

"About the Author" and "At the Caprock"

**Grades 3-8:** Read "About the Author" and "At the Caprock" and answer the following questions. Write the letter of the correct answer on the blank next to each question number.

_____1. The author tells us that this story's setting is in _____.
   a. WWII
   b. The Great Depression
   c. England
   d. Georgia

_____2. The author's father is the youngest of _____ children.
   a. 11
   b. 3
   c. 1
   d. 2

*King of the Hill*

_____3. These stories take place when the Bedfords are _____.

   a. shopkeepers

   b. miners

   c. farmers

   d. circus performers

_____4. Who helps Papa drive?

   a. Ira and Benji

   b. Mary and Mama

   c. Troy and LD

   d. LD's wife and Jewel

_____5. Which two family members stay behind to work when the family leaves for Paducah, Texas?

   a. Ira and Fritz

   b. LD and his wife

   c. Mary and Jewel

   d. AT and Billie

**Directions Grades 3-5:** Match the following terms with their meanings in the story by writing the letter of the correct answer in the space beside the number.

\_\_\_1. The Great Depression       a. trade goods instead of using money

___2. Indian Territory

___3. ingenuity

___4. odd jobs

___5. Model-T

___6. Caprock Escarpment

___7. gullies

___8. barter

b. a lot of people lose their jobs

c. a place where high plains and low plains meet

d. resembles a big ditch

e. using imagination to solve problems

f. land given to the Native Americans

g. unrelated tasks; temporary work

h. an early 1900s truck or car

*King of the Hill*

## "Pulling Cotton"

**Directions Grades 6-8:** After reading the chapter, answer the following questions by writing FACT or FICTION in the blank next to the numbered items. Write the whole word.

**Directions Grades 3-5:** Third grade teachers may want to change the directions to TRUE or FALSE and/or instruct the students to answer the questions following a class discussion.

_____1. Papa knows Benji will volunteer to pick cotton.

_____2. "Picking Cotton" is yanking off the entire boll and stuffing it in the sack.

_____3. The more cotton Benji pulls, the more he gets paid.

_____4. The seeds are used to make oil.

_____5. Ira helps Benji when he falls behind the others pulling cotton.

_____6. Benji writes down his own weights as he pulls cotton.

_____7. Benji can remember the exact amount pulled by each family member at the end of each day.

_____8. Jewel is the fastest cotton puller.

_____9. The Bedfords drive the Model-T to neighboring farms to work.

_____10. In 1932, the children start to school late in the year, because they have to work in the fields.

*King of the Hill*

## "The Three R's"

**Directions for Grades 6-8:** Answer the following questions as you read the chapter. Be sure to spell words correctly and write neatly.

1. _____ defends Benji from a bully on the school bus.

2. The _____ school is in a ten-room, two-story brick building.

3. When the recess bell rings, Benji thinks it is _____.

4. Benji is moved from _____ to _____ first because he can already read and add and subtract.

5. Benji has gotten good with _____ by keeping track of rows and bags in the cotton fields.

6. Benji isn't sure how he learned to _____.

7. The boys' nightly ritual involves _____.

8. Benji and Ira save pennies to buy _____ (book).

9. Benji drops the _____ jar while he is imitating the teacher.

10. Ira uses the "Vinegar Story" to _____ Benji.

11. _____ always knew about the vinegar jar breaking, because Benji charged both jars of vinegar and mama had to pay for them at the end of the month.

**Directions Grades 3-5:** Choose the correct answer and write it in the blank provided for each question.

1. _____ defends Benji from a bully on the school bus.
    a. The red-headed girl
    b. The red-headed boy
    C. Jewel
    d. Ira

2. Benji attends the _____ school.
    a. Bedford
    b. Caprock
    c. Dickens
    d. Farmer

3. When the recess bell rings, Benji thinks it is____.
    a. the end of the school day
    b. recess
    c. lunch
    d. time for math

4. Benji isn't sure how he learned to _____.
    a. read
    b. walk
    c. work math problems
    d. play football

5. The boys' nightly ritual involves _____.
    a. shooting baskets
    b. cleaning their room
    c. praying
    d. telling stories

6. _____ always knew about the vinegar jar breaking, because Benji charged both jars of vinegar and mama had to pay for them at the end of the month.
    a. Jewell
    b. Mama
    c. Troy
    d. Coach

"Third Time's the Charm"

**Directions Grades 6-8:** After reading the chapter, answer the following questions using complete sentences. Some answers will require a short paragraph. Remember to obey all the punctuation and capitalization rules.

1. Explain the title of this chapter. Keep in mind that the family lived at the Stevens place for one season, the Gilstrap Place for one year, and now, they are headed for the Reynolds Place.

2. Why is Papa having such a difficult time driving the family cart in this chapter?

3. For what two things does the family use the cellar at the Gilstrap Place?

4. How does Benji get Ira to call off the "Vinegar-Vinegar" deal?

5. Why does Benji hate crossing the field of pie melons?

7. Why does Benji feel safe crossing the pie melon field with Papa?

8. How might Papa use the twine he collected? You will need to use what you know about how the family solves problems that arise and your own imagination to answer this question.

*King of the Hill*

**Directions for Grades 3-5:** After the students have read and discussed the chapter, the teacher will divide the students into teams of three or four. Each team will be given one of the following questions. Assign roles to each team member. The reader will read the section which deals with the question aloud to the others as they follow along. The scribe will jot down each team member's idea about how to answer the question. The reporter will look up any words that are unfamiliar and share with the group. The editor (may have two roles if group of 3) will write the final copy of answer to share with class. The group will choose a spokesperson to report what they have written to the class.

1. Why is Papa having such a difficult time driving the family cart in this chapter?

2. The family uses the cellar at the Gilstrap Place to protect themselves and their food. What do we do to protect ourselves and our food today?

2. How does Benji get Ira to call off the "Vinegar-Vinegar" deal?

3. Benji hates crossing the field of pie melons. Why does Benji feel safe crossing the pie melon field with Papa?

4. How might Papa use the twine he collected? You will need to use what you know about how the family solves problems that arise and your own imagination to answer this question.

"Elbow Grease"

**Directions Grades 3-8:** As you read the chapter, answer the following questions by choosing the correct answer for each question and writing the letter of the correct answer beside the number.

\_\_\_\_\_1. The home at the Reynolds Place uses the sun and \_\_\_\_\_ for lighting.

    a. electricity

    b. gas

    c. candles

    d. kerosene lamps

\_\_\_\_\_2. The Aladdin Lamp company offers a \_\_\_\_\_ to anyone who can show them a better lamp.

    a. $1000.00 prize

    b. good horse

    c. year's supply of oil

    d. new lamp

\_\_\_\_\_3. The wood stove often \_\_\_\_\_.

    a. burns cow chips

    b. burns mesquite stumps

    c. catches fire

    d. a-c

_____4. The family uses catalogues and dried corn cobs for _____.

    a. fuel in the stove

    b. toilet paper

    c. padding

    d. none of the above

_____5. Washing and ironing clothes is done using _____.

    a. iron pot

    b. washing board

    c. homemade soap

    d. a-c

    e. none of the above

_____6. The family only bathes by _____ on Saturday.

    a. immersion

    b. swimming

    c. spraying one another

    d. none of the above

*Nelda Bedford Gaydou*

## "No Job Too Big or Small" and "King of the Hill"

**Directions Grades 6-8:** To test recall, the teacher may use this matching activity as a quick quiz, class discussion guide, small group activity, or activity to be completed individually.

**Directions Grades 3-5:** To test recall, the teacher may use this matching activity as a class discussion guide, small group activity, or activity to be completed individually as students read the chapter.

_____1. Benji

_____2. cultivator

_____3. dowser

_____4. Papa

_____5. farmer

_____6. iceman

_____7. ice boxes

_____8. ice cream

_____9. money

_____10. 50-pound cotton bag

a. resembles a giant bicycle

b. tools are hooks, tongs, picks

c. drives farm equipment

d. water finder

e. owns all farm animals

f. needs drip pans

g. sewing fabric

h. scarce

i. Benji's favorite treat

j. hired to dig a well

*King of the Hill*

## "Changes" and "Excursions"

**Directions Grades 3-8:** Read the two chapters and match the numbered term on the left with the correct statement on the right by writing the letter of the correct answer on the blank beside the numbered item.

_____1. L.D.'s family

_____2. home

_____3. Papa

_____4. Mama

_____5. Benji

_____6. Ira and Benji

_____7. A.T. and Benji

_____8. Jewel and J.P.

_____9. George, Crawford, Henry

_____10. George

a. learns to drive before Ira

b. willing to walk 15 miles home

c. moves to Spur

d. don't have a quarter for YMCA

e. victims of a hit and run

f. where Mama and Papa are

g. may have stolen family relics

h. Tuberculosis

i. one-fourth Choctaw

j. takes charge when Papa dies

## "Twists and Turns"

**Directions Grades 6-8:** After reading the chapter, answer the following questions by writing FACT or FICTION in the blank next to the numbered items. Write the whole word.

**Directions Grades 3-5:** Teacher may want to change directions to read "TRUE or FALSE."

_____1. Mama and the family manage the farming with no outside help after Papa dies.

_____2. Benji swallows tobacco and decides he really likes it a lot.

_____3. The family moves to New Mexico when the crops are harvested.

_____4. Benji is enrolled in 6th grade at Mi Casita where many of his family have attended.

_____5. After the move, Benji and his family are surrounded by strangers.

_____6. In New Mexico, the family has electricity, running water, and indoor bathrooms.

_____7. Benji only agrees to work at one job in the drugstore on weekends.

_____8. At the end of the story, Benji is relieved that his life in Texas in finally over.

# ABOUT THE AUTHOR

Although her mother and father hail from West Texas and Eastern New Mexico, Nelda Bedford Gaydou was born and raised in Argentina. Her childhood home is described in two biographical works about her missionary parents—*To the Ends of the Earth: High Plains to Patagonia* (winner of the 2017 International Book Award for General Biography) and *From Sea to Sea: River Plate to Lake Michigan*.

The author's mother taught her to read in English before starting public school in Spanish, and she's been hooked on reading and writing ever since. Married, with three children, four grandchildren (pictured with her above) and three Labrador Retrievers, she lives in the mountains of central Argentina.

Gaydou's next work is *The Color of the Flame*, a family memoir on dementia. Upcoming projects include another book of Benji stories (this time about town life during the Great Depression in Clovis, New Mexico) and Spanish versions of the biographies.

***Progressive Rising Phoenix Press*** is an independent publisher. We offer wholesale discounts and multiple binding options with no minimum purchases for schools, libraries, book clubs, and retail vendors. We also offer rewards for libraries, schools, independent book stores, and book clubs. Please visit our website and wholesale discount page at:

## www.ProgressiveRisingPhoenix.com

***Progressive Rising Phoenix Press*** is adding new titles from our award-winning authors on a regular basis and has books in the following genres: children's chapter books and picture books, middle grade, young adult, action adventure, mystery and suspense, contemporary fiction, romance, historical fiction, fantasy, science fiction, and non-fiction covering a variety of topics from military to inspirational to biographical. Visit our website to see our updated catalogue of titles.

www.ingramcontent.com/pod-product-compliance
Lightning Source LLC
LaVergne TN
LVHW040743250326
834688LV00031B/425